SCIENCE DARES YOU!

Build a
ROOM ALARM

And 16 more
electrifying projects!

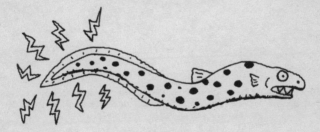

by Sandra Markle
Illustrated by Eric Brace

SCHOLASTIC INC.

New York   Toronto   London   Auckland   Sydney
Mexico City   New Delhi   Hong Kong   Buenos Aires

For dear friends Don and Pam Roberts. —S.M.

*For Erick Johnson, the best high school science teacher
a guy could ask for... I mean art teacher...
The best high school art teacher a guy could ask for. —E.B.*

The author would like to thank Dr. Richard Lane, Senior Lecturer,
Department of Electrical and Computer Engineering, University of Canterbury,
New Zealand, for sharing his expertise and enthusiasm.
As always, a special thanks to Skip Jeffery, for his help and support.

ISBN 0-439-44432-2

12 11 10 9 8 7 6 5 4 3 2   3 4 5 6 7 8/0
                                                              40
Printed in the U.S.A.
First printing, February 2003
Design by Jennifer Rinaldi Windau

SCIENCE DARES YOU TO . . .

Note to Parents and Teachers: The books in the Science Dares You! series encourage children to wonder why and to investigate to find out. While they have fun exploring, young readers discover basic science concepts related to each book's theme. They also develop problem-solving strategies they can use when tackling any challenge.

In this book, children tackle challenges that help them develop an understanding of electricity and electrical circuits. "Electricity in circuits can produce light, heat, sound, and magnetic effects. Electrical circuits require a complete loop through which an electrical current can pass." (National Science Education Standards as identified by the National Academy of Sciences.)

SCIENCE DARES YOU TO
GET CHARGED UP!

WHAT IF you could make paper **jump** into the air as if by magic, make a lightbulb glow in your hand without plugging it into a wall socket, or build a burglar alarm to let you know when somebody enters your bedroom? Believe it or not, you can do all these things—*and lots more*—when you tackle the dares in this book. All you need is some creativity, a little help from Science, and an amazing **force**:

ELECTRICITY.

The Basics

First, you need to know something about electricity. Electricity is a collection of charged bits called *electrons*. Electrons are normally parts of *atoms*. Everything in the universe is made of atoms, but these building blocks are too tiny for your eyes to see. Electrons are even tinier.

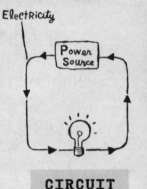

Sometimes, electrons are knocked out of their atoms. Then those loose electrons may bump into other atoms and free still more electrons.

Free electrons can be collected in one place or moved from one place to another. When the electrons are just in one place, the charged bits form *static electricity*. When the electrons are flowing from one place to another, the charged bits form an *electric current*. Sometimes this current may flow through a pathway, such as a wire. Then the electricity is said to flow in a *circuit*. When the electricity flows from a source, through a pathway, and back to that source, the circuit is called a *complete circuit*.

STAY SAFE!

Electricity can be strong enough to be dangerous, so you should always be careful and ask your parents' permission before taking the dares. You'll be using the electrical charge produced by something called a dry cell, or D-cell. These are often called batteries. D-cells produce enough electricity to do the projects in this book, and they're safe for you to work with.

be careful

Never, ever plug any of your experiments into a wall plug, a light socket, or any other electrical outlet!

You're almost ready to get charged up and put electricity to work! But first, here are some tips that will help you meet each science challenge.

HELPFUL HINTS

Brainstorm ways to tackle the challenge. Use the clues provided to help you think of possibilities. Then list three to five things you could try.

Choose which ideas would be most likely to work. Don't forget to check with an adult to be sure your idea is safe for you to test.

Test your idea. Then read over the suggested way to meet the challenge. Try it, too. Then decide if this approach provides some ideas you might use to modify and improve your solution.

Now you're ready to get charged up. Good luck—and don't forget to have fun!

DEPOSIT ELECTRICITY ON A BALLOON

Don't worry! You can meet this challenge
with a little help from science.

Clues:

✘ To deposit electrons, you'll need to find a source of electrons. Could you knock electrons loose? How could rubbing help you meet the dare?

✘ Have you ever heard a crackling noise while pulling on a wool sweater? What do you think caused that noise? How could it help you?

Take the Dare!

You'll need:

Inflated rubber balloon
Woolen cloth

1. Rub the balloon quickly back and forth five times with the wool. Congratulations—you've just completed the dare!

2. Prove to yourself that you've deposited electricity on the balloon by bringing the spot you rubbed close to your bare arm. The balloon should be just above, but not touching, the hairs on your arm.

3. Watch as you move the balloon. You should see the hairs move, too. You may even experience a slight tingling sensation.

What Happened?

Wool is made up of atoms, just like everything else. When you rubbed the wool against the rubber balloon, you knocked free some of the wool atoms' electrons. Then those loose electrons collected on the surface of the balloon. Remember, electricity that builds up in one place is called **static electricity**.

WOW! Even the ancient Greeks observed static electricity. They discovered they could produce this charge by rubbing silk on amber (hardened tree sap). The word **electricity** comes from the Greek word **elektron**, meaning amber.

DOUBLE DARE #1

What else could you rub on a balloon, besides wool, to give it an electric charge? Stumped? You can find useful strategies for all the double dares at the back of the book.

MAKE PAPER JUMP

This dare may sound tough, but you can do it.
Check out the clues for ideas.

Clues:

✗ Tie a string to an inflated balloon and hang it from a ruler stretched over the side of a table. Charge up a second inflated balloon, as you did in the first dare. Then bring the charged surface close to the suspended balloon. You'll see the suspended balloon move to meet the charged balloon. How might this reaction help you meet the challenge?

✗ Position your arm so the hairs are close to a sheet of notebook paper. Your hairs won't move and you won't feel a tingle this time. Do you think the paper has a charge?

12

Take the Dare!

You'll need:

Sheet of notebook paper
Table
Inflated rubber balloon
Woolen cloth

1. Tear off a piece of paper the size of a quarter, and place it on the table.

2. Next, build up a static electric charge on a balloon by rubbing it back and forth on the wool.

3. Watch carefully as you slowly bring the charged part of the balloon close to the paper. The paper will appear to jump up. Then the paper will stick to the balloon.

Sit...

Heel...

Jump???

What Happened?

Objects can have two types of charges: positive and negative. Opposite charges attract—that means positive and negative particles are pulled together. Like charges repel, which means that negative particles push other negative particles away, and positive particles push other particles away. Because the paper and balloon had opposite charges, they were attracted to each other. And, because the paper was so light, that pull was enough to move it.

How long does the paper stick to the balloon? Tie a string to the balloon and attach it to a ruler so the balloon is suspended over the side of a table. Check frequently to find out how much time passes before the paper drops off the balloon. Could rubbing the balloon on the wool more times make the paper stick longer? Science dares you to design an experiment to find out.

USE ELECTRICITY TO MOVE A BALLOON

Before you start brainstorming how to tackle this challenge, check out the clues.

Clues:

✗ **What happens if you charge both balloons and then bring one toward the other? Try it!**

✗ **Do the charged balloons have to touch before they interact? Find out.**

Take the Dare!

You'll need:

2 identical inflated rubber balloons
Woolen cloth
Table

1. Rub one balloon back and forth against the wool. Turn it slowly, and keep on rubbing until you've rubbed all the way around the balloon. Set that balloon on the table.

2. Pick up the other balloon, and rub it against the wool.

3. Hold the charged part of that balloon just above the one on the table, and move it in small circles. The balloon on the table should move.

4. Try guiding it toward the opposite side of the table. If the balloon stops rolling, quickly recharge the one in your hand by rubbing it on the wool. Then continue.

What Happened?

When you rubbed both balloons, you gave each an identical charge. When you brought the charged balloons together, the two like charges pushed away from each other. And, because the inflated balloon was so light, this push was enough to make it move.

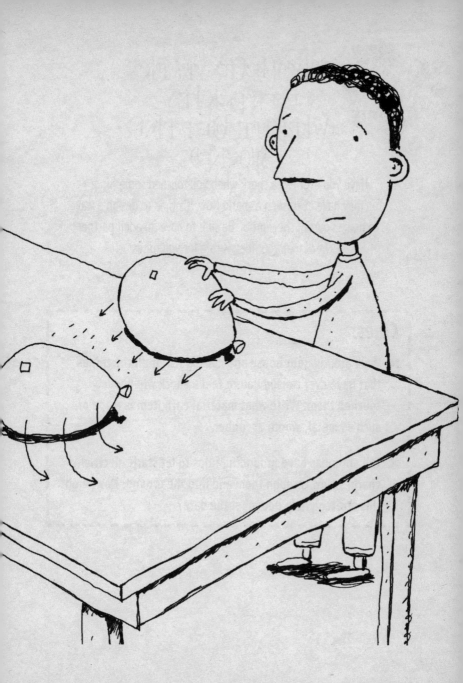

DISCHARGE STATIC ELECTRICITY WITHOUT GETTING SHOCKED

Have you ever felt a shock when you touched something? You may have even seen a spark! Now, it's time to design a way to make yourself shockproof. Be sure to have an adult partner check that your idea is safe for you to test.

Clues:

✘ Walk around your house and make a list of all the things that have ever caused you to feel a shock when you touched them. Write what material each item is made of, such as metal, wood, or rubber.

✘ Tall antennas have grounding lines to let static electricity charges flow through them and into the ground. How might this strategy help you meet the dare?

Take the Dare!

You'll need:

Steel paper clips
Aluminum foil wires

1. Follow the directions on p. 23 to make foil wires. You'll need them for a lot of the dares in this book.

2. Clip foil wires together to make one long enough to reach from your hand to the floor when you're standing up.

3. Walk across the floor dragging the foil wire.

4. While still holding the foil wire, touch a metal doorknob. You won't feel a shock because you've just met the dare!

What Happened?

When you walk across a rug, a static electric charge builds up on your shoes. Then touching certain objects, such as a metal doorknob, cause the static electricity to suddenly flow through you as it's discharged. That's when you feel a shock. But if you never build up a static electric charge, there isn't anything to discharge. The aluminum foil provides a pathway that the electrons can easily move through. So as quickly as an electric charge collects on your shoes, it flows up your body, through the foil wire, and back to the carpet. And that means no shocks for you!

ALUMINUM FOIL

MAKE FOIL WIRES

You'll need:

Aluminum foil
Transparent tape
Scissors

1. Place a 9" x 12" sheet of foil dull side up.

2. Stick strips of tape down the length of the foil, leaving a small gap between each row.

3. Cut along each side of the tape to create foil ribbons.

4. Fold each ribbon in half lengthwise, with the tape inside. Crease the folds to press the two sides together.

5. If you need to use longer aluminum foil wires, use steel paper clips to connect two or more together. If you need a shorter wire, cut off a piece.

A Historic Dare

INVENTOR BENJAMIN FRANKLIN was intrigued by electricity. He was convinced lightning was like small static electric charges and wanted to prove it. So in 1752, he launched a homemade kite into a storm (don't try this yourself!). Soon, a charge traveled down the damp kite string, and a spark jumped to his knuckles. Ben Franklin had proven lightning was a discharge of static electricity, but he was also lucky he wasn't actually struck by lightning. A single bolt produces enough energy to light a 100-watt bulb for three months. Of course, a lightning bolt appears much brighter than a lightbulb. That's because when lightning strikes, all of this energy is delivered in a fraction of a second.

Franklin used what he'd discovered to invent the lightning rod. This protects buildings from lightning the same way the foil wire drag shockproofed you. A lightning rod is a metal rod placed at the highest point on a building. It is connected to a wire that stretches to the ground.

LIGHT UP A LIGHTBULB WITHOUT PLUGGING IT IN

Sound like you need magic? You don't! You can do it with
a little help from science and a special source of electricity.

Clues:

✗ A portable radio runs on electricity, but it doesn't plug into
a wall socket. Ask an adult to show you what supplies a
portable radio with electricity.

✗ Look closely at a D-cell battery. How could you use a foil
wire to make the electrons produced in the D-cell flow
through a complete circuit?

✗ Now, look closely at a flashlight bulb. How could you make
it part of a complete circuit with a D-cell?

Electricity

Power Source

Circuit

Take the Dare!

You'll need:

Transparent tape
Aluminum foil wire
D-cell (battery)
1.5-volt flashlight bulb
Small rubber band

1. Tape one end of your foil wire to the indented end of the D-cell. This is called the negative terminal. Your battery probably has little "+" and "–" signs on it. The "–" end marks the negative terminal.

2. Wrap the other end of the wire around the bulb's metal base, and secure with the rubber band.

3. While you hold the D-cell in your hand, touch the tip of the lightbulb's base to the knob end of the battery. This is the positive terminal, and it is probably marked by a "+" sign. Presto! The bulb lights, and you've met the dare.

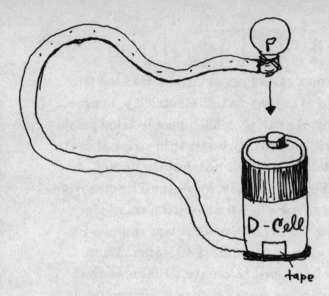

D-Cell

tape

What Happened?

The D-cell was your source of electricity. The
foil wire created a complete circuit, or pathway,
that carried a flow of electrons from the D-cell
through the flashlight bulb. And that made the
lightbulb glow.

If you look closely at an unlit bulb, you can
discover what makes it glow. Inside the bulb,
there is a very thin wire, the filament. Because it's
so thin, electrons passing through it have to
squeeze through. This causes friction, which heats
up the filament. It gets hot enough to glow.

A Historic Dare

LOTS OF DIFFERENT PEOPLE have tackled the challenge of trying to use electricity to produce light. As early as 1802, people tried passing an electric current through thin strips of metal. The metal glowed red hot, but it quickly melted. Finally, in 1879, inventor Thomas Alva Edison created a lightbulb with a small piece of cotton coated in carbon. This was called a filament. It glowed for almost 40 hours. Then, Edison set to work to create a filament that would last even longer before it burned up. In all, he tested more than six thousand different kinds of materials from all over the world. At last, Edison found a type of bamboo with fibers that made long-lasting filaments for his lightbulbs. These filaments gave a dull, yellowish light. Other inventors tried other materials, but these were rare and too expensive for everyday use. Finally, in 1911, inventors used tungsten to create long-lasting filaments that gave a bright, white light. And tungsten is still used today to make most lightbulbs.

Science dares you to find a way to focus the light beam from a handheld light. Look closely at a flashlight to see how it focuses light.

WOW! Here you can peek inside a D-cell to see
how it produces electricity. The D-cell is made up of a chemical
paste with a carbon rod down the center. The knob end is called the
positive terminal. The indented end is called the negative terminal.
A chemical reaction in the paste frees electrons. The electrons remain inside
the D-cell until the positive and negative terminals are connected in a complete
circuit. Then the electrons flow into the carbon rod, through the circuit, and back
into the D-cell. Along the way, some of the electricity may be used up to light a
lightbulb, make a radio play, or power up another electrical device.
The D-cell will not produce new electrons indefinitely. As the chemical reaction
happens, the chemicals themselves change. Eventually, the chemical reaction
stops. Then the D-cell is "dead." And it's time to plug a new D-cell into the circuit.

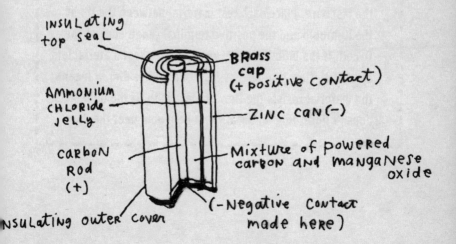

INSULating
top seaL

BRass
cap
(+ positive coNtact)

AMMONIUM
CHLORide
JeLLy

ZINC caN (-)

CARBON
Rod
(+)

Mixture of powered
carBoN aNd maNgaNese
oxide

NSULatiNg outer cover

(- Negative coNtact
made here)

MAKE ELECTRICITY TRAVEL WITHOUT A WIRE

Explore your house to find materials that electricity
will flow through easily. Use the clues to launch your search.

Clues:

✗ You know electricity flows through the aluminum foil
wires. What kind of material is aluminum — wood, metal,
glass, or rock? Could a similar kind of material help you
meet this dare?

✗ Test materials with the lightbulb circuit you made to meet
the last dare. Place each test material between the tip of
the lightbulb and the positive terminal (knob end) of the
D-cell. If the bulb is bright, you know the test material lets
electricity flow through easily. If the bulb is dim, it means
the material resists the flow of electricity. If the bulb
doesn't light, that material won't help you meet the dare.

Take the Dare!

You'll need:

- **Yardstick or meter stick**
- **Aluminum foil wires**
- **Handheld light from the previous dare**
- **Small rubber band**
- **Transparent tape**
- **Assortment of copper pennies, steel paper clips, metal keys, an empty metal soda can, and a metal spoon**
- **Adult partner**

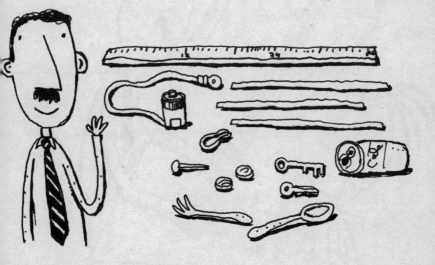

1. Lay the yardstick or meter stick on the table.

2. Clip enough foil wires together to make a wire 3 feet (1 meter) long.

3. Place one end of this wire over the D-cell's positive terminal (knob end) and tape in place.

4. Use tape to attach a copper penny or a steel paper clip to one end of the yardstick. Make sure the tape only covers half of the metal item.

5. Arrange more items that made a good pathway for electricity along the ruler. Be sure each item touches the next one in line.

6. Finally, prove that you've met the dare. Have your adult partner hold the D-cell, negative terminal (indented end) down, on the first item taped on the ruler.

7. Wrap the free end of the wire taped to the D-cell's positive terminal around the lightbulb's metal base.

8. Touch the tip of the base to the final item in the chain. As long as all of the items in the chain are touching, the bulb should light!

What Happened?

Some materials let electrons move through them easily. These are called *conductors*. Metals, such as steel, iron, gold, and aluminum are good conductors. Other materials resist electron flow. These are called *insulators*. Glass, rubber, and wax are examples of good insulators. As long as the items you arrange in a line are all good conductors, they will form a complete circuit and light the bulb.

2.)

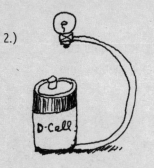

assemble parts

4.)

rate brightness

9.)

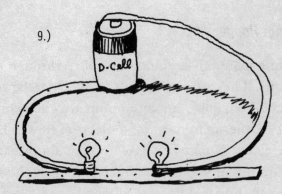

rate brightness with both bulbs.

DIM A BULB

Can you figure out a way to make
a normally bright light become dimmer?
The clues will get you started.

Clues:

Look closely at the circuit you made to light a bulb (pages 25–27).

✘ What happens to make the bulb light? Could you decrease the amount of electricity flowing through the whole circuit?

✘ How could you decrease the amount of electricity reaching the bulb?

Take the Dare!

You'll need:

> **3 aluminum foil wires**
> **D-cell**
> **Two 1.5-volt flashlight bulbs**
> **2 small rubber bands**
> **Transparent tape**

1. Tape the end of one foil wire to the D-cell's negative terminal (indented end).

2. Wrap the other end of that wire around one of the bulbs. Secure with a small rubber band.

3. Check the brightness of the bulb in this circuit by touching the tip of the bulb's base to the D-cell's positive terminal (knob end).

4. Rate the brightness on a scale of one to five, with five being the brightest.

5. Take the bulb's tip off the D-cell's terminal.

6. Wrap one end of the other two foil wires around the second flashlight bulb's base and secure with a rubber band.

7. Wrap the free end of this wire over the positive terminal of the D-cell and tape in place.

8. Lay the third foil wire on a tabletop, and smooth flat.

9. Touch the tips of both of the bulbs' bases to the wire on the table. Both bulbs should glow.

Once both bulbs are lit, rate the brightness of each bulb on the same one-to-five scale. Congratulations! You met the dare because neither bulb is as bright as the single bulb alone.

TROUBLESHOOTING:

× If either one of your bulbs is not glowing, check all of your connection points.

× Check the second bulb alone to be sure it's working.

What Happened?

You already know why a bulb lights. Electricity flowing through a circuit passes through the bulb's filament. In the circuit you just built, electricity must flow through a series of bulbs. This kind of circuit is called a *series circuit*. The current reaches the first bulb, and then what's left goes on to the next. Neither bulb in the series gets as much current as it would if it was in the circuit alone. So neither bulb glows as brightly.

SERIES CIRCUIT

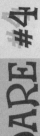

Now science dares you to make a single
bulb in a circuit glow more
brightly than usual.

WOW!

Electric eels have chains of special cells that act like D-cells
wired in a series. In fact, a big electric eel can produce pulses
of electricity five times stronger than what's available from
your home's electrical outlets! Electric eels use weak pulses
like radar to help them sense obstacles when they're swim-
ming through muddy water. They use strong jolts to kill prey
and repel predators. A thick layer of insulating fat keeps
an electric eel from shocking itself.

CONNECT TWO BULBS SO ONE STAYS LIT EVEN IF THE OTHER BURNS OUT

Don't worry! You can meet this dare,
too, with a little help from science.
The clues below will start you brainstorming.

Clues:

✘ Look at the picture below. How many different pathways
can you find for the electric current to travel? How might
it help to have more than one pathway?

✘ How might giving each bulb its own connection to the
D-cell battery help you meet this challenge?

Take the Dare!

You'll need:

Transparent tape
3 aluminum foil wires
D-cell
Table
Two 1.5-volt flashlight bulbs
2 small rubber bands
Partner

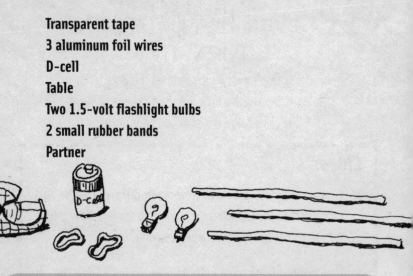

1. Tape the end of one foil wire to the D-cell's negative terminal (indented end).

2. Set the D-cell, negative terminal down, on a table, and smooth the wire out flat.

3. Tape the second wire to the middle of the third wire.

4. Have your partner press one end of the third wire to the D-cell's positive terminal (knob end). Then tape it in place.

5. Pick up the free end of one of the wires attached to the D-cell's positive terminal. Wrap it around the base of one of the lightbulbs and secure it with a rubber band.

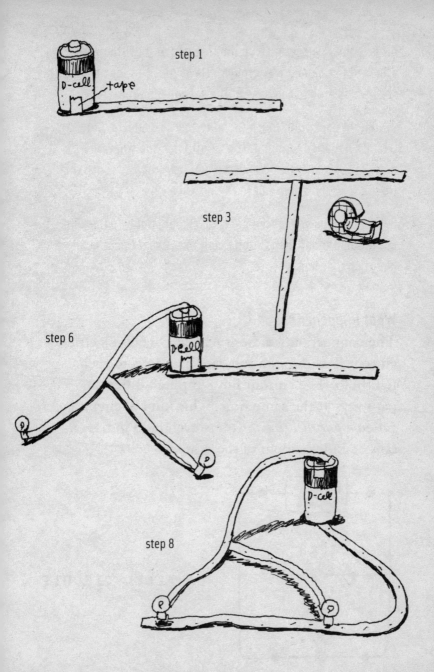

step 1

D-cell

tape

step 3

step 6

D-cell

step 8

D-cell

6. Have your partner pick up the free end of the other wire attached to the positive terminal. Have your partner wrap and secure this around the base of the second lightbulb.

7. To light your bulb, touch its tip to the wire attached to the D-cell's negative terminal. (Be careful that the two wires don't touch in the process.) Have your partner also touch the tip of the second bulb's base to this same wire.

8. To prove you've met the dare, touch both bulbs to the wire at the same time. Then lift one bulb to see that the other keeps on glowing.

What Happened?

The connection you built let the D-cell's electric current flow through separate pathways to each lightbulb. The current flows through different pathways at the same time. This kind of circuit is called a *parallel circuit*. It lets each bulb in the circuit be independent of the others.

PARALLEL CIRCUIT

Find a way to short-circuit the parallel circuit you just created. Electricity always travels in the easiest and shortest pathway. So when the electric current bypasses the lightbulb in the circuit, it's called a *short circuit*. You'll know you've succeeded in creating a short circuit when both bulbs go out at once.

WOW!

• Imagine having nearly 6,000 bulbs hooked together in a circuit! That's what lights up just one of the dazzling floats in Disney World's electric parade. The bulbs lighting these floats are connected in parallel circuits so a burned-out bulb won't spoil the show.

BuILD A ROOM ALARM

How can you keep people (like sneaky younger brothers or sisters) out of your stuff? If you could make a battery-powered radio turn on when someone came in, there would be no more surprise visitors! So how could you set up a radio to do that? Let the clues help you brainstorm an invention. Check with an adult to be sure your idea is safe to test.

Clues:

✗ Look at the batteries inside a battery-powered radio. How might you interrupt the flow of electricity from the batteries?

✗ How could you use your bedroom door to trigger the radio to turn on?

Take the Dare!

You'll need:

Scissors
3" x 5" index card
Hole punch
6 feet (about 2 meters) of strong string
Battery-powered radio that uses two or more D-cells
Transparent tape

1. Cut off about a fourth of the index card.

2. Punch a hole close to one end of that small piece of the card.

3. Tie one end of the string to the card through the hole.

4. Remove the battery panel on the radio to expose the D-cells.

5. Tape the D-cells in place.

6. Switch the radio on to be sure it still plays, turn the volume all the way up, and then switch the radio off again.

7. Slip the end of the card without the hole between two of the D-cells.

8. Push it in just far enough to cover the positive terminal. If the D-cells are side by side, slide your card in between one D-cell's positive terminal and the metal on the inner wall of the battery panel.

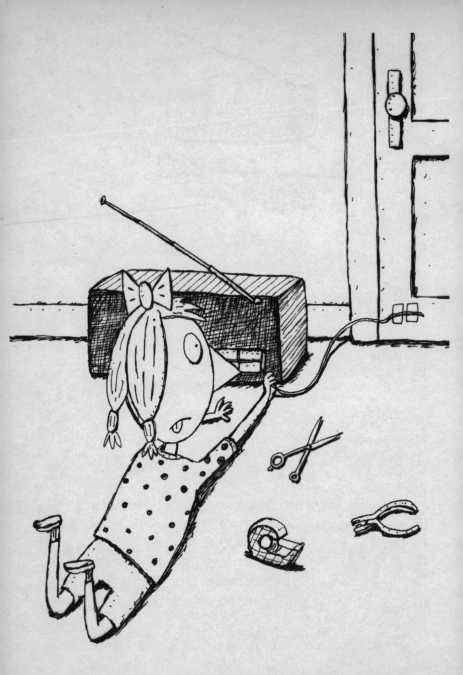

9. Switch on the radio to check that it doesn't play. If the radio comes on, the card is not covering the positive terminal. Turn the radio off again and adjust as needed.

10. Set the radio in the hall outside your bedroom door, and tape the free end of the string to the edge of the door just above the floor.

11. Move the radio away from the door until the string is not quite tight.

12. Test your burglar alarm by opening the bedroom door. The card should be pulled out of the radio, and the radio should turn on. If this doesn't happen, adjust the string or placement of the radio until opening the door yanks the index card out of the radio.

What Happened?

You've just created a *switch*, a device that controls whether an electric current flows through a circuit. Inserting the card interrupts the electric current flowing through the radio's circuits and switches it off. Removing this barrier lets the electric current flow again, switching the radio on.

MAKE A BULB LIGHT UP WITH A PUSH OF YOUR FINGER

Now that you've created one kind of switch,
science dares you to make another. Can you make a switch that you
can push to complete a circuit? The clues will get you started.

Clues:

✗ Look at the series of D-cells powering your radio.
How could you force the D-cells' electric current through
a separate side circuit, before it moves on to the
radio's circuits?

✗ Look again at the series circuit you created to dim a bulb
(pages 35–37). How is this circuit like a switch? How could
this sort of connection help you design a pressure switch?

materials and supplies

Take the Dare!

You'll need:

Scissors
Aluminum foil
2 aluminum foil wires
Stapler
2 flexible paper plates
Table
Transparent tape
D-cell
Flashlight bulb
Adult partner

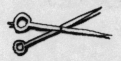

1. Cut two pieces of aluminum foil about as big as a 3'' x 5'' index card.

2. Fold the foil pieces in half—shiny side in.

3. Place the end of one wire inside each foil packet, and staple to anchor it in place.

4. Set the two paper plates, flat bottom down, on the table.

5. Place one foil packet in the middle of each plate. Anchor them with tape.

6. Set one plate on top of the other so the foil packets are inside.

7. Twist the top plate until its wire comes out at a right angle.

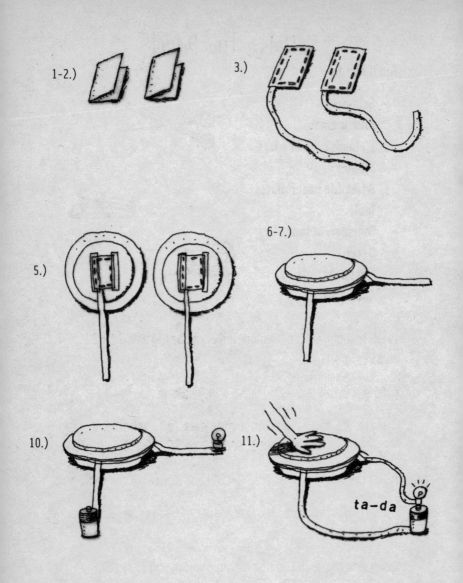

1-2.)

3.)

5.)

6-7.)

10.)

11.)

ta-da

8. Tape the sides of the plates together.

9. Set the negative terminal (indented end) of the D-cell on the bottom plate's wire.

10. Have your partner wrap the free end of the other foil wire around the base of the lightbulb and touch it to the tip of the base of the D-cell's positive terminal (knob end).

11. Press down on the middle of the top plate. Presto! The bulb will light.

What Happened?

To make this switch, you've interrupted the flow of electricity through the aluminum foil wire pathway. Pressing the two aluminum foil packets together completes the circuit. It lets electric current flow through the lightbulb.

WOW!

In 1795, Italian scientist Alessandro Volta made the first successful chemical battery. Unlike today's D-cells, it used a series of zinc and silver plates separated by pieces of paper or cloth dipped in salt water. Imagine trying to power up your portable radio with one of those batteries!

BLOW A FUSE

Before you can blow a fuse, you need to make one.
Look through the clues to understand what a fuse is
and how it works. Then start inventing.

Clues:

✗ A fuse is a safety device that will open an electric circuit,
which will stop the flow of electricity. It blows, or breaks
the circuit, when the current gets dangerously strong.

✗ How could using D-cells in a series circuit help blow a fuse?

✗ Metal can make a good fuse because, if the piece of metal
gets hot enough, it melts. And that opens the circuit.
Would it be better to build a fuse using metal that melts at
a low temperature or a high temperature?

A Historic Dare

FUSES WERE invented to keep circuits from
carrying such a powerful electric current that
the wires melted, starting a fire. No one is quite
sure who invented the first fuse. But the first patent
for a fuse was granted to Thomas Edison in 1880.
In the early days, each electric lamp was fitted
with its own separate fuse.

Take the Dare!

You'll need:

2 D-cells
Transparent tape
2 pennies
Marking pen
2 aluminum foil wires
Scissors
Steel wool
3" x 5" index card or piece of cardboard
Table
1.5-volt flashlight bulb
Adult partner

1. Stack the two D-cells so the positive terminal of the bottom one is against the negative terminal of the top one. Secure with tape.

2. Place two pennies on the card so that only a paper clip turned on its edge can fit between them.

3. Anchor the outer edge of the penny on the right with tape. Mark an "X" under this penny.

4. Place one of the foil wires in the center of a second piece of tape and set it aside.

5. Snip off a two-inch (five-centimeter) piece of steel wool.

1-4.)

5.)

7.)

10.)

11.)

12.)

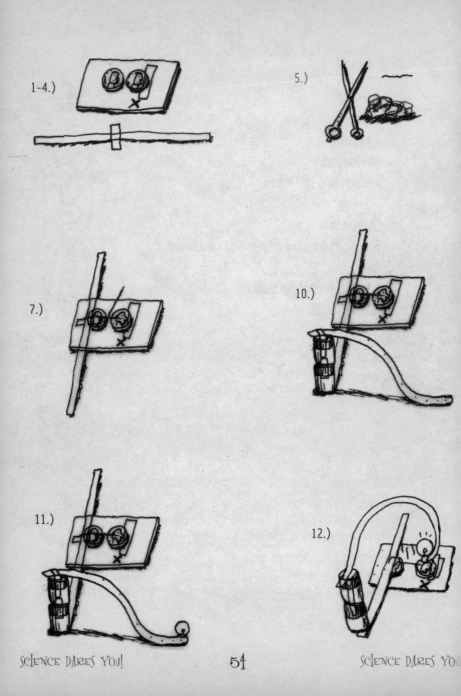

6. Stretch the steel wool across the tops of the two pennies to form a straight line. Have your adult partner tape the steel wool to the right-hand penny.

7. Have your partner use the tape with the steel wool attached to anchor the other end of the steel wool to the left-hand penny.

8. Place the index card on a table. Flatten out one of the aluminum foil wires.

9. Place the free end of the second wire over the positive terminal of the D-cell stack, and secure it with tape.

10. Set the D-cell stack, negative terminal down, on the foil wire that's lying on the table.

11. To activate your fuse, have your adult partner wrap the end of the foil wire taped to the positive terminal around the lightbulb's base.

12. Have your partner touch the tip of the bulb's base to the penny above the X. The bulb will light briefly, and then it will go out. This is the result of the wire melting. This means the fuse is blown, opening the circuit. So you've met your dare.

What Happened?

Like a lightbulb's filament, the steel wool resists the flow of electricity. So it heats up. Eventually, the steel wool melts, opening the circuit.

USE ELECTRICITY TO LIFT AT LEAST 10 STEEL PAPER CLIPS

Not sure what to invent to meet this challenge?
Use the clues to figure it out.

Clues:

✗ Steel is a metal. How is metal different from other materials like plastic or paper?

✗ Check in books or on the Internet to find out how electricity could be used to create a magnetic field of attraction.

WOW!

In the future, electromagnets could transform how people travel. By 2003, Shanghai is scheduled to have the first commercial maglev, or magnetic levitation, train. Maglev trains are lifted above their tracks, guided and propelled along by electromagnetic forces. Since there's no friction between the wheels and the track to slow it down, a maglev train is expected to be able to reach speeds of more than 310 miles (500 kilometers) per hour!

Take the Dare!

You'll need:

> **10 standard-sized steel paper clips**
> **Table**
> **Scissors**
> **3 feet (about 1 meter) of fine-gauge**
>   **insulated copper wire**
> **Steel or iron nail (16-penny size)**
> **6-volt lantern battery**
> **Adult partner**

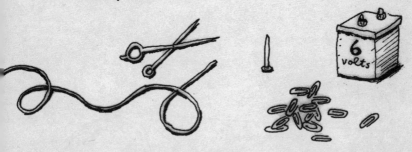

1. Place the paper clips in a pile on the table.

2. Have your adult partner use the scissors to strip about an inch (2.5 centimeters) of insulation off each end of the wire.

3. Wind the wire around the nail 25 times. Slide the coils together on the nail.

4. Have your adult partner hook one end of the wire through each of the lantern battery's terminals. Don't touch the exposed copper ends of the wire, because they can get hot!

1-2.)

3.)

4.)

6 volts

5.)

6 volts

5. To pick up the paper clips, touch the tip of the nail to the pile of paper clips.

6. Count how many paper clips you can lift in a bunch to see if you've met the dare. Then, immediately unhook one end of the wire to keep it from getting hot.

If you were unable to lift at least 10 paper clips, you can make your invention stronger by adding 25 more coils of wire around the nail. Then try to pick up the paper clips again. How many more can you pick up?

What Happened?

The device you created to attract the metal is called an *electromagnet*. The electric current passing through the nail makes it act just like a magnet. So the nail is able to attract the steel paper clips. The more coils you wind around the nail, the stronger the electromagnet becomes. Unlike a magnet, an electromagnet is only temporary. The magnetic field of attraction only lasts as long as an electric current is running through it.

#1. You can use silk and your hair to deposit an electric charge on the balloon. You'll probably find other materials that work, too.

#2. Use two identical inflated rubber balloons tied to strings. Rub one balloon five times with a square of woolen cloth. Rub the other balloon 10 times. Use both to pick up the paper, and then suspend the balloons side by side. Make a list of all of the conditions surrounding the balloons that could affect the results of your experiment, including air temperature and humidity. Check at regular intervals to see how long the paper will stick to each balloon. Repeat this test at least two more times to be sure the results you discover are likely to happen every time. Then conduct another test, rubbing one balloon 10 times and the other 20 times.

You should discover that increasing the charge on the balloon increases how long the paper will stick, but it doesn't necessarily double the time.

#3. You may come up with another idea, but you can construct a poster-board cone lined with shiny aluminum foil to place around the bulb.

#4. Attach two D-cells in a series circuit to power up one lightbulb. This will increase the amount of electric current passing through the lightbulb and make it glow more brightly.

#5. Place an aluminum wire so that it touches both the wire connected to the D-cell's negative terminal and one connected to its positive terminal. Be sure this wire is between the D-cell and the first lightbulb. This will form a short circuit that cuts out the lightbulb.

DARE YOURSELF!

Congratulations! You've successfully met the dares presented in this book. You're not finished, though. Now, science dares you to use what you've discovered about electricity: how it can be generated, how it can flow through a circuit, and how it can be used to produce heat, light, and a magnetic force field. So create your own challenges. Then brainstorm and plan experiments. Check with an adult partner to be sure what you want to try is safe to test. And let science help you meet all the dares you can dream up!

SCIENCE WORDS

ATOM Tiny particles that make up everything in the universe.

CIRCUIT A complete pathway that electricity can move through.

CONDUCTOR A type of material, such as steel, that electricity can flow through easily.

ELECTRIC CURRENT Free-moving electrons that flow through a pathway.

ELECTROMAGNET A magnetic field created by electricity flowing through a coil of wire wrapped around a piece of iron or steel.

ELECTRON A tiny, negatively charged particle that is part of an atom.

FUSE A safety device that keeps too strong an electric current from flowing through a circuit. It melts when the current gets dangerously strong.

INSULATOR A type of material, such as glass, that electricity can't flow through easily.

PARALLEL CIRCUIT A circuit in which each appliance or device is attached separately to the source of electricity.

SERIES CIRCUIT A circuit in which electricity must flow through each appliance or device one after the other to complete the pathway.

STATIC ELECTRICITY A buildup of an electrical charge in one location.

SWITCH A device that makes it possible to easily open and close a circuit, controlling the flow of an electric current.